THE SLOVAK RECIPES

From My Grandmother's Kitchen

Written & Illustrated by Darryl Stefanik

Edited by Mark Stefanik

This little cookbook is for all of Helena Zubercova–Stefanik's children here and in heaven.

Preface

There are some foods that shape our vivid memories of childhood. They are the dishes that brought everyone to the table together knowing that each of us would soon be enjoying a delicious slice, bowl, or plate of something truly special. It was by no means haute cuisine with expensive ingredients, but food that made you feel you were being hugged tightly by the ones that loved you dearly. For many years I have craved these Slovak dishes from my childhood but have not been able to find them in any restaurant or cook them with my own family. Fortunately, Darryl Stefanik has been a documentarian and guardian of the Stefanik's Slovak culinary traditions. He has kept these precious recipes alive by making them year after year and carefully recording the techniques he has honed over time. It is by no means an easy task bringing recipes from the old country to life with so little being written down and such imprecise measurements of "a little of this" and a "handful of that." The Slovak Recipes from My Grandmother's Kitchen clearly presents these recipes with detailed instructions in a way that both novice and advanced cooks can follow. Adding color to the flavors, the author's delightful illustrations bring these dishes to life with loving energy and playful movement. Mark Stefanik's layout and organization creates a touching homage to my great-grandmother, Helena Stefanik, including priceless photographs of her at the stove. These details make this cookbook a beautiful tribute to her love for her family and her talents as a cook. This collection of delicious recipes will surely be passed down through future generations, keeping our Slovak culinary traditions alive and offering each of us a chance to enjoy the foods of our childhood once again.

Justin Stefanik

Helena Zubercova-Stefanik
10 Campbell Avenue, Hamilton, Ontario
Canada

Her favorite flower was the rose, the national flower of Slovakia

Introduction

(T)y Granny, Helena Zubercova-Stefanik, showed her love for all her grandchildren in many ways. In the winter, she made sure we were always wearing an undershirt underneath our regular one so that we would be warmer. At her kitchen table, quietly drinking from a cup of tea, she would make eye contact and pretend to spit in your direction three times. This old world tradition served as a reminder of her faith and that of the Trinity; the Father, the Son and the Holy Ghost. It reassured her (and us) that we were protected, honored and important.

Very often my Granny expressed her love by gently holding your face with her aged hands, kissing your forehead and thanking God for you, for every moment and everything in her life.

Most of all, our dearest Granny showed her love by preparing traditional Slovak cuisine, both savoury and sweet, not just on holidays like Christmas and Easter, but every time we were with her. This little cookbook, *The Slovak Recipes From My Grandmother's Kitchen* was written in her memory and from my heart and soul.

The book only features the recipes I best remember from experiences in the kitchen and at the dinner table with her. Oh, there are other dishes that she prepared for me like sour garlic soup and a lettuce soup that I have forgotten how to make.

In 1930, my beloved Granny was almost twenty-one when she said goodbye to Kokava, the small village and home in Slovakia. She arrived in Canada with these now treasured recipes in her heart and in her soul. Granny loved to cook. She loved to eat and would often be overheard saying, "To je delicious!"

Darryl R. Stefanik was born and raised in Hamilton, Ontario. He received his Bachelor's Degree in Fine Arts and Art History from McMaster University and a Master's Degree in Theological Studies.

For over 25 years, Darryl has served as a Lutheran Pastor in a small country parish. Darryl loves spending time with his wife Cornelia, family and friends. He and Cornelia have two children, Anastasia and Franz-Paul, along with five grandchildren; Bauer, Beckam, Beau, Jaxon and Xander.

In his leisure time Darryl enjoys gardening and lovingly maintaining a lemon tree. Darryl avidly attends the theatre and knows how to tap dance. Over the years he baked hundreds of tortes (in Granny's honor) for his family and friends both near and far. Darryl and Cornelia reside in Ridgeway, Ontario, a small hamlet near Niagara Falls.

Užite si jedlo

slané jedlá

Cabbage or Bean Soup

4 cups shredded cabbage or 4 cups green or yellow
  beans trimmed & cut in half.
2 potatoes peeled & cut in cubes
  2 tomatoes peeled & quartered
1 cup of milk
1/4 cup lard or bacon fat
1/4 cup flour
1 small onion sliced
  salt & pepper to taste
  vinegar to taste

In a medium size soup pot with at least 8 cups
of water, boil cabbage (or beans) with potatoes
and tomatoes until all is tender. season
with salt.
In a non-stick frying plan heat up lard (or fat)
onions and flour and cook until it forms
a golden roux. Adjust with more fat if necessary.
add roux to soup pot and simmer until
soup thickens. Add milk season with
more salt, pepper and add vinegar to
taste. serve warm with some cream.

Clear Chicken Soup

1 small whole chicken-
2 small oinions peeled + whole
4 stalks celery cut in half
4 carrots peeled and whole
10 pepper corns
1 bay leaf
salt to taste.

In a large soup place chicken, oinions, celery, carrots, pepper corns, bay leaf and cover well with cold water. Place on stove and bring soup to boil and then simmer for at least an hour. Skimm off extra fat that floats to surface. Remove cooked chicken and cool. Season soup generously with salt. Serve soup with a floating carrot and cut meat from chicken. Serve also with some Noodles (see recipe) or Thin Pancakes rolled up and cut into strips (see recipe).

(Halauphi)
Cabbage Rolls

1 small head of cabbage
1/2 lb ground beef
1/2 lb ground pork
1 large onion (1/4 cup fat)
2 tsps. paprika
salt & pepper to taste.
2 large cans of tomato juice
2 cups cooked rice.

Core & steam whole cabbage in a pot with
1/2 water. Set aside & cool. In a bowl mix
beef, pork, rice, season well with salt and
pepper. In a small frying pan fry diced
onion in fat, season with paprika and
add to meat & rice mixture. Mix well.
Peel leaves of cabbge and fill with
meat mixture and place in a deep
baking dish (be sure to roll up leaves
gently & tucking the ends into their centre
forming a little bundle. If rib of leaf is
too tough remove with a knife. Pour one
can of tomato juice over rolls & cover
with foil rap. Bake for 1 hour 1/2 topping
with extra tomato juice. Serve rolls with
sour cream. For Stuffed Peppers, hollow peppers
and fill with meat mixture instead. (oven temp. 400°F).

halušky

4 large (new) potatoes peeled
2½ cups flour
1 tablespoon salt
8 thick slices of bacon cut into
   small cubes
3 cup grated white Old Cheddar Cheese
   (Bryndza is traditional)

In a mixing bowl grate potatoes on the finest
section of a box grater (wet & puree-like)
You could easily use a food processor.
Mix flour and salt into potatoe mixture.
The dough should be sticky. Add more flour
if too wet or a little water if too dry.
Bring a pot of water to boil.
Place enough dough onto small cutting board
With a paring knife cut little pieces of
dough into the boiling water. Simmer
gently until noodles float. With a slotted
spoon collect noodles and place in large
mixing bowl. Repeat until all noodles
have been cooked. Cover noodles with
cheese. Fry bacon until very crisp & fat is
rendered. Pour fat over cheese & noodles.
Mix well and add Sour Cream. Season
with salt & pepper, garnish with bacon.
Serve immediately. 2 large servings
or 4 small.

Ham

Boil Ham (with bone in) in a pot
with 1/3 filled with water for
at least 1 hour. Drain and then
bake ham in 400°F oven for
another hour. Glaze with
apricot Jam (with a little
brandy or rum). Serve warm
or cold.

Duck

Bake well seasoned duck (
plenty of salt and pepper) in
a shallow baking pan uncovered
for at least 2 hours. (350°F)
Drain off fat periodically + save.
Serve warm or cold.

Chicken
(Kuraci Paprikas)

Lightly dust in flour 4-6 boneless chicken thighs.
Salt & Pepper. Fry chicken in heavy bottomed
pot until brown. Add 1 tablespoon paprika
and 1 diced onion. Add 2 cups of chicken
stock or broth and bake for 1 hour at 400°F
with a covered lid. Add 2 tablespoons of
flour + thicken sauce while continuing to bake.
Wisk in 1 cup of sour cream. Serve with noodles

Kapusta
(Kapustnica)

In a heavy bottom pot
fry 1 small diced onion
in 1/4 cup bacon fat.
Saute with 1/2 teaspoon
caraway seeds. Stir in 1
heaping tablespoon flour
and brown lightly. Add
1 jar of good Sauerkraut,
1 bay leave and simmer
until thick. Season
with pepper and serve
as a side dish.

Sauerkr.

Noodles

— ooo —

Needle:

3 cups flour

2 eggs

1/2 cups water

Mix eggs and water in a bowl.
Add flour + mix with fork
Knead mixture in bowl
until elastic. Cut into 3
pieces. Cover with a tea towel
and let stand 30 minutes.
Roll each piece of dough as
thin as possible. Let each
rolled sheet of dough dry out
a few minutes. Roll up each
sheet of dough and carefully cut
into desired width of noodles.
Cook in well salted boiling
water 4 to 5 minutes.
Drain

Noodles and Cabbage
(hlávkové zelé dušené)

Prepare noodle recipe

In a heavy skillet heat 1/4 cup bacon fat, fry 1 sliced onion & 4 cups thinly sliced cabbage until tender. Add salt & pepper to taste and serve with sour cream.

Pancakes
(Livance)

1 package dry yeast
2 tablespoons sugar
2½ - 2¼ cups flour
2 cups milk (warmed)
1 or 2 egg yolks
½ teaspoon of lemon peel (zested)
⅓ cup butter
(jam or cinnamon)

In a medium size bowl mix yeast
sugar and warm milk. Let rise 5-10 minutes
Add egg(s), salt, lemon peel Beat well
Let rise 30 minutes. Heat heavy bottom frying
pan & brush with a little extra butter
or oil or lard Spoon batter into pan and
make 3-4 inch pancakes - turn to brown
on both sides, Spread with jam or cinnamon
Sugar. You could also dust with icing sugar.

Pierogies

(Pierogi)

2 large potatoes
1 cups old cheddar cheese (white) shredded
2 eggs
1 tablespoon oil
3 cups flour
salt & pepper.
1/2 cup melted butter.

In a small pot boil peeled & quartered potatoes until tender. Drain & mash with cheese. Salt & pepper to taste. Let cool.

In a bowl mix flour, eggs, oil together until it forms a nice dough. Knead gently in bowl and let rest. (you may add a little water if dough is too dry). Divide dough into 2 and roll out each dough very thinly on a floured board or counter. Using a solid drinking glass (or cookie cutter) cut out dough into rounds and fill each with at least 1 tsp. of potato mixture. Fold each round & pinch tight. In a large pot of boiling water drop pierogies and gently simmer them until they float (3 min.) Drain and place in frying pan and melted butter serve with fried onions (optional) and sour cream.

Granny preparing halusky, a favorite with all 9 of the grandchildren.
Photo circa 1970s courtesy of the Stefanik Family Archive

Doughnuts (Koblihy)

1 package of dry yeast
1 1/2 cups of milk or cream (warmed)
3 tablespoons butter
1/4 cup sugar
4-5 egg yolks
4 cups flour
(1-2 tablespoons rum or brandy ⋆optional)
pinch of salt
2-3 cups oil for frying.

In a large bowl mix yeast with warm milk/cream and sugar. Let rise 5-10 minutes. Add soften butter, egg yolks to yeast mixture. Mix in flour + salt. Knead dough in bowl-dust with flour and let rise for 45 minutes. On a lightly floured board roll out dough 1/5 in thick. Cut out circles with 3 in cutter or use the top of a solid cup or glass. With a 1 inch cutter cut out centres of circles (or leave whole if you want to fill doughnuts with jam) Place circles of dough on lightly floured cloth and let rise 1/2 hour. Heat oil in heavy bottom pot or skillet. Fry doughnuts 2 minutes on each side. Remove from oil and let drain on paper towel. Dust doughnuts with icing sugar or fill solid doughnuts with seedless raspberry or plumb jam (roll in sugar).

(Egg Bread)
Koláč

4 cups flour
1 package dry yeast
2 tablespoons sugar
3 large tablespoons sour cream
3 large tablespoons soft butter
4 egg yolks
1 cup warm water
1 cup warm milk.
½ cup golden raisins
1½ tsp of salt.

In a large bowl mix together water, milk
sugar & dry yeast. Let rise for 5 minutes.
Mix in all other ingredients and knead
dough on board — Put dough back into bowl
punch down & let rise 1 hour. Punch down
dough & shape into 2 large balls on board.
Place dough into spring form pans. Cover
with cloth & let rise 1½ hours. Bake
dough in a 375° oven 1 hour. Test with
tooth pick to make sure bread is
baked in centre. Cool & serve with butter
& Jam.

harotsa

(fánky, mašličky, bozie milosti)

3 cups flour
3 eggs
1 tablespoon sugar
2 tablespoons sour cream (heaping)
2 tablespoons vegetable oil
2 packages of pure lard
1 cup icing sugar

In a mixing bowl combine all ingredients and
knead dough in bowl for a few minutes.
If too dry add a little water. Dough should
be elastic and not sticky. Cover bowl with
towel + let rest 1 hour. Divide dough in
two and shape each piece into rounds.
On a flat surface lightly dusted with flour
and using a rolling pin, roll out round dough
until very, very thin. With a fluted
cutting pastry wheel cut dough into
various shapes. Square, rectangles, triangles etc.
With wheel make a small slit in the centre
of each shape. In a heavy frying pan or
cast iron pot melt lard until hot and
lightly fry dough shapes until golden
and crisp. You can even fashion dough
shapes into bowties, butterfly shapes etc.
Carefully put fried dough in a large
bowl and dust generously with icing
sugar. Fried dough + sugar!

Lattice Pie
(Koláč Mřížkový)

2 3/4 cup flour
1/3 cup sugar
1 cup butter (soften)
2 egg yolks
1/2 tsp grated lemon peel
1/2 tsp vanilla
Jam or Poppy Seed Filling

Mix all ingredients together
Shape into 2 discs let rest
1/2 hour.

On a floured board roll out dough
until pie crust thin.

Place dough in spring form pan
and trim to fit.

Spread with Jam (apricot) or
poppy seed mixture. (Poppy Seed Filling)

With remaining dough cut thin
strips and lattice these over
the dough and jam pie. With
an egg wash brush top of pie
sprinkle with sugar and bake
at 35°F for 40 min. or until
golden. Cool and release from
spring form. Cut into triangles
or squares. (Wedges as well).

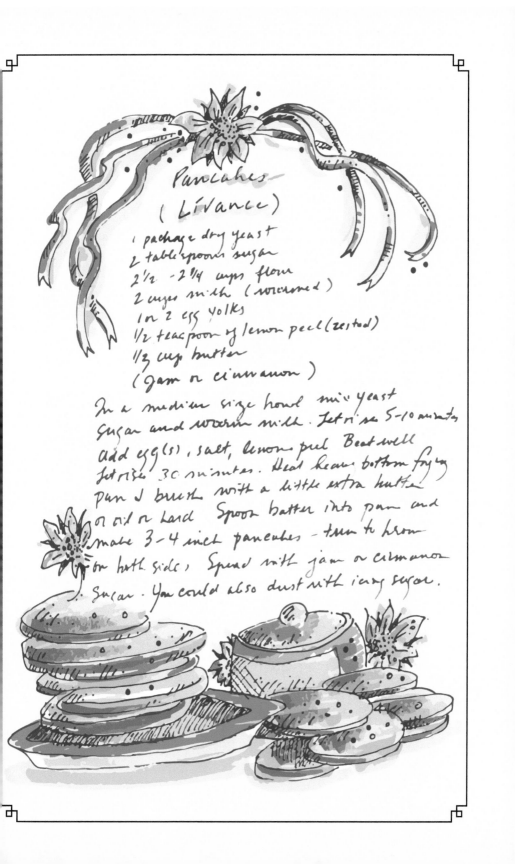

Pancakes
(Lívance)

1 package dry yeast
2 tablespoons sugar
2 1/2 - 2 1/4 cups flour
2 cups milk (warmed)
1 or 2 egg yolks
1/2 teaspoon of lemon peel (zested)
1/3 cup butter
(jam or cinnamon)

In a medium size bowl mix yeast
sugar and warm milk. Let rise 5-10 minutes
add egg(s), salt, lemon peel. Beat well
Let rise 30 minutes. Heat heavy bottom frying
pan & brush with a little extra butter
or oil or lard. Spoon batter into pan and
make 3-4 inch pancakes - turn to brown
on both sides. Spread with jam or cinnamon
Sugar. You could also dust with icing sugar.

Poppy Seed Filling
(Maková Nádivka)

2 cups ground poppy seed
3/4 cup milk
2/3 cup sugar
2 tablespoons butter
1 teaspoon vanilla
1/2 teaspoon cinnamon (optional)
1/2 teaspoon grated lemon peel
2 tablespoons jam (any flavour)
1 egg separated.

Simmer in pot poppy seeds
and all other ingredients except
egg whites. Stir constantly.
Let cool + stir in whipped egg
white. Use for Poppy Seed Roll
or Lattice Pie.

poppy seed roll

3½ cups flour
1/4 cup icing sugar (powdered)
2 egg yolks
1 package of yeast
pinch of salt
1 stick butter plus 3 (melted)
    tablespoons butter
3/4 cup warm milk. (1 cup also
    for poppy seed mixture)
2 cups poppy seeds (or ground walnuts)
1 tablespoon oil
1 tablespoon vanilla
1/2 cup golden raisins.

In a stand mixer bowl with an attached dough hook mix flour, icing
sugar, egg yolks, yeast, salt, butter, milk - knead well. Let
dough rise until double. In a small pot warm extra milk, oil
powdered sugar and vanilla. In a blender grind in batches poppy seeds
icing seeds are opened and resemble wet coffee grounds.
Mix poppy seeds with milk mixture & bring to boil. Add raisins
and let cool. On a flat surface divide dough into 2 pieces
and roll out thin. Spread poppyseed mixture over dough
almost to the edges. Roll up doughs and place on baking
pan lined with parchment - let rise for at least
1 hour and ½. Bake rolls at 375°F for 30-40 minutes.
(You may want to brush rolls with a light egg wash.

strudel dough

2⅓ cups flour   ½ cup warm water
pinch salt   ½ teaspoon vinegar
1 egg, beaten   1 tablespoon lard, melted

In a bowl mix all ingredients until it forms
a dough. Knead dough until smooth and
elastic. Let it rest with a cover on it. 30 min.

Cover a table with a clean cloth and sprinkled
with flour. Place dough in centre and sprinkle
with flour, roll out to ⅛th in. thick. With back
of your hands clenched fists, start stretching
dough working from centre until paper thin.
Be carefull not to tear dough.

apple strudel

Brush thin dough with melted butter (½ cup) sprinkle
with bread crumbs. Spread peeled & sliced apples
at one end of the dough and sprinkle soft sugar (¾ cup)
mixed with cinnamon (½ tsp) and raisins (⅓ cup)
Using cloth roll up dough, and brush with butter
as you form strudel. Place on baking sheet,
generously butter and bake strudel for 30
minutes (350°F) Dust with icing sugar.

cherry strudel

substitute sour or sweet cherries that
are pitted & follow same instructions
for apple strudel.

Thin Pancakes
(Palačinky)

2 eggs
pinch of salt
3 tablespoons sugar
2 cups milk
2 cups flour
1/4 cup butter (melted)

In a bowl mix all ingredients together with a whisk. Reserve some melted butter to grease frying pan. Let the batter rest for 30 minutes. Heat heavy bottom frying pan (or nonstick pan) and brush with remaining butter. With a ladle pour batter in pan enough to make a paper thin pancake. Brown both sides and dust with icing sugar or spread with jam.

Walnut Cake (Torte)
(Dort Oříchový)

12 eggs, separated
12 tablespoons sugar (heaping with European soup spoon)
6 heaping tablespoons finely ground walnuts
6 heaping tablespoons flour
2 teaspoons baking powder
1 teaspoon vanilla
pinch of salt.

Beat egg whites until stiff. Beat egg yolks, sugar, vanilla until double in volume. Mix flour, baking powder, salt and nuts into yolk batter. Gently fold in egg whites. Pour into greased or buttered & floured spring forms (2 small or 1 large). Bake at 400°F for 5 minutes and then reduce the heat to 375°F for 30 minutes until cakes test clean with toothpick. Remove cakes from pans and let cool on a rack. Cut rounds into layers fill with whipping cream, butter cream & fresh fruit. Cover entire cake with butter cream and decorate with additional whipping cream and a few left over ground walnuts.

The Zuberec family house
Slovenskeho Narodneho Povstania 379/9
Kokava nad Rimavicou, Slovakia

Notes:

Notes:

Notes:

Notes:

Helena Zuberova-Stefanik
Undated confirmation photo/courtesy of the Stefanik Family Archive

CPSIA information can be obtained
at www.ICGtesting.com
Printed in the USA
LVHW070024191120
671950LV00011BA/24/J